NATIONAL GEOGRAPHIC
Forces of Nature

GENRE Folk Tale

Read to find out how Paul and Babe changed the land.

# PAUL BUNYAN AND BABE THE BLUE OX

RETOLD BY ROGER BACH
ILLUSTRATED BY ROBB MOMMAERTS

BABE THE BLUE OX
PAUL BUNYAN
LUMBERJACKS WERE BUSY IN THE 1800S. AT THIS TIME, THE UNITED STATES WAS GROWING FASTER THAN CORN IN IOWA. A LARGE AMOUNT OF LUMBER WAS NEEDED TO BUILD FACTORIES, BRIDGES, AND RAILROADS. LUMBERJACKS LIVED IN LOGGING CAMPS THAT WERE OFTEN FAR FROM TOWNS.
DURING THE LONG WINTERS, THEY ENTERTAINED EACH OTHER WITH STORIES. SOME TOLD TALES ABOUT A GIANT LUMBERJACK NAMED PAUL BUNYAN. THE STORIES WERE LATER PUBLISHED AND NEW TALES WERE ADDED.

IN THE YEAR OF TWO WINTERS . . .
IT WAS SO COLD, THE LUMBERJACKS IN PAUL'S CAMP COULDN'T GO OUTSIDE WITHOUT THEIR NOSES TURNING BLUE. LUCKILY PAUL COULD BEAR THE BITTER COLD. OTHERWISE BABE MIGHT NOT HAVE BEEN RESCUED THAT DAY IN MINNESOTA.
WHAT ARE THOSE, BEANPOLES? I'VE NEVER SEEN THOSE BEFORE.
SNORT
YOU POOR BABE, YOU'RE COLDER THAN THE SHADY SIDE OF AN ICEBERG. I'LL CALL YOU "BABE THE BLUE OX."

THAT SPRING, BABE JUST GREW AND GREW.
I GUESS APPLE FLAPJACKS ARE OFF THE MENU!
YUM!
THE LUMBERJACKS FOUND NEW WAYS FOR BABE TO HELP WITH CHORES.
I HOPE THEY GIVE ME A SNACK BEFORE THESE DRY.
IT TOOK OLE THE BLACKSMITH A YEAR TO FORGE BABE'S "OX SHOES." EACH SHOE WEIGHED MORE THAN 12 MEN.
WHEN BABE WAS FULLY GROWN, HE COULD EASILY PULL 50 LOGS. AT FIRST THE LUMBERJACKS DIDN'T RECOGNIZE THE SOUND OF BABE'S STOMPING.
IS THAT THUNDER?

PAUL'S WAGON-WHEEL PANCAKES REQUIRED A PAN BIG ENOUGH TO **BOAST** ABOUT. THE PAN WAS HEAVIER THAN A RAILROAD CAR.
TO GREASE THE PAN, MEN SKATED ACROSS IT ON SLABS OF BUTTER. THEN SOMEONE PULLED A ROPE TO POUR BATTER INTO THE PAN.
BE CAREFUL, BOYS! DON'T COOK YOUR FEET!
WATCH OUT!
WHOA!

PAUL AND BABE FORM THE 10,000 LAKES . . .
IN THE SUMMER, PAUL AND BABE ROAMED THE OUTDOORS AND PLAYED GAMES. ONCE PAUL TRIED TO TEACH BABE HOW TO PLAY FETCH.
TRY TO CATCH MY LONG TOSS!
THEN BABE DECIDED TO TEACH PAUL HOW TO WRESTLE.
PAUL AND BABE WRESTLED UP AND DOWN MINNESOTA. NOBODY EVER FOUND OUT WHO WON.
NOW I HAVE YOU!
I DOUBT IT!
LATER A MIGHTY THUNDERSTORM FLOODED THE **LANDFORMS** THEY LEFT BEHIND. THAT'S HOW MINNESOTA'S 10,000 LAKES WERE FORMED.

PAUL MAKES THE GREAT LAKES . . .
DURING THE SUMMER OF NO RAIN, ALL 10,000 LAKES DRIED UP. PAUL AND BABE CROSSED THE **BORDER** INTO WISCONSIN TO FIND WATER.
THE ONLY WAY TO FIND WATER WAS TO DIG FOR IT.
PAUL AND BABE DUG FIVE HUGE HOLES BORDERING EIGHT STATES AND CANADA. BUT THEY DIDN'T FIND A SINGLE DROP.
PARDON MY BOASTING, BUT I CAN OUT-DIG AN ARMY OF GOPHERS.
PAUL GAVE IT ONE LAST TRY, SWINGING HIS AX WITH SUCH **FORCE** THE GROUND SHOOK. WATER SHOT UP LIKE A GEYSER.
THE WATER FILLED THE FIVE HUGE HOLES, AND THAT'S HOW THE GREAT LAKES WERE FORMED.

PAUL AND BABE FORM THE MISSISSIPPI . . .
ONCE PAUL WANTED TO ICE THE LOGGING ROADS. HE MADE A BARREL SO ENORMOUS IT TOOK HALF A DAY TO WALK AROUND IT. PAUL FILLED IT WITH WATER FROM LAKE SUPERIOR.
PAUL COULD BARELY LIFT THE BARREL, YET HE PERSUADED BABE TO HAUL IT.
YOU'LL GET AN ORCHARD'S WORTH OF APPLES FOR THIS.
ONLY 30 MILES MORE!
SNORT!
BABE TRIPPED. THE BARREL CRASHED AND BROKE OPEN.
HUMPH!
THE WATER FLOWED UNTIL IT REACHED THE SEA, AND THAT'S HOW THE MISSISSIPPI RIVER WAS FORMED.

PAUL FORMS THE GRAND CANYON . . .
PAUL AND BABE HEADED OUT WEST, TURNING SOUTH IN SOUTH DAKOTA. AT THE ARIZONA BORDER, IT WAS HOT ENOUGH TO FRY A FLAPJACK ON PAUL'S AX.
I HAVEN'T SEEN LAND THIS PARCHED SINCE THE SUMMER OF NO RAIN.
WATCH YOUR STEP, BABE. YOU DON'T WANT TO TRIP ON A CANYON.
I MISS THE SNOW.
PAUL AND BABE WEREN'T USED TO THE EXTREME HEAT.
I WISH THIS AX WEREN'T SO HEAVY. ALTHOUGH I'M STRONG, THE SUN IS STRONGER.

**Check In** What were the forces of nature in these tales?

**GENRE Science Article** **Read to find out** how water shapes Earth's surface.

# Water's Might

by Brian Phelps

Water can be one of nature's mightiest **forces.** Rivers, oceans, and sheets of ice build and destroy **landforms.** Water shapes Earth's surface. It can wear down mountains and carve out valleys. It can move boulders that are bigger than a house. These changes can happen quickly or take thousands of years.

Spencer Glacier in Alaska's Kenai Mountains

# Earth's Icy Past

Earth looked much different 20,000 years ago. Almost one-third of Earth's land was covered by **glaciers.** Glaciers are giant, slow-moving sheets of ice. They form where snow builds up year after year. Slowly the weight of the top layers of snow squeezes the bottom layers into ice. This heavy ice pushes out and flows downhill. Some glaciers can move several meters a day.

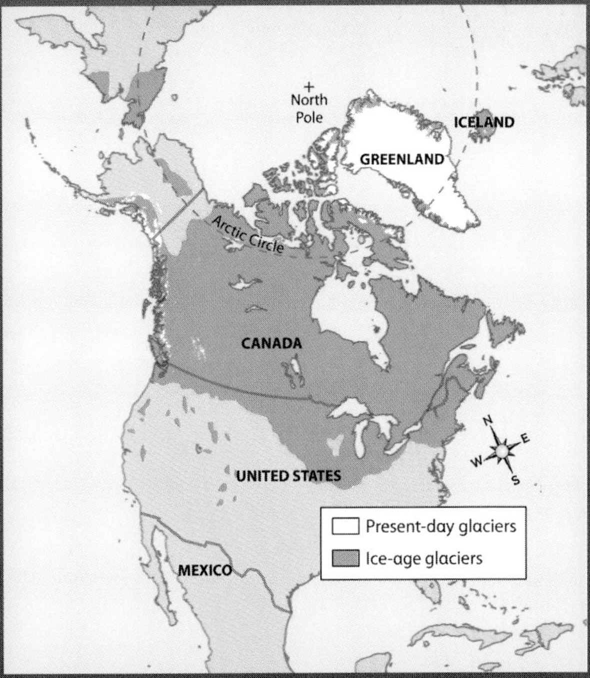


Glaciers spread and shrank several times during the last ice age. In some places, the ice was more than 3 kilometers (almost 2 miles) thick! Today's glaciers cover Antarctica, most of Greenland, and many high mountains.

## The Great Lakes

Over time, the huge ice-age glaciers caused major changes in North America. As the glaciers moved, their size and weight eroded the land under them. **Erosion** is the movement of rock and soil from one place to another. The glaciers caused erosion by carrying large amounts of sediment, or loose material. This loose material includes soil, sand, gravel, and rocks.

When the glaciers began to melt, they dropped the sediment. **Deposition** is the laying down of sediment in a new place. Ice-age glaciers deposited enough sediment to form hills and other landforms. The melting ice also released fresh water. The water filled low spots, forming the Great Lakes. Together the Great Lakes make up the largest surface area of fresh water on Earth.

### HOW DID LAKE MICHIGAN FORM?

**1 MILLION YEARS AGO**

The area now covered by Lake Michigan was a lowland. It had valleys and rivers.

**20,000 YEARS AGO**

Erosion by earlier glaciers had gouged out the land to form a basin. A basin is a very wide area that is deeper than the surrounding land.

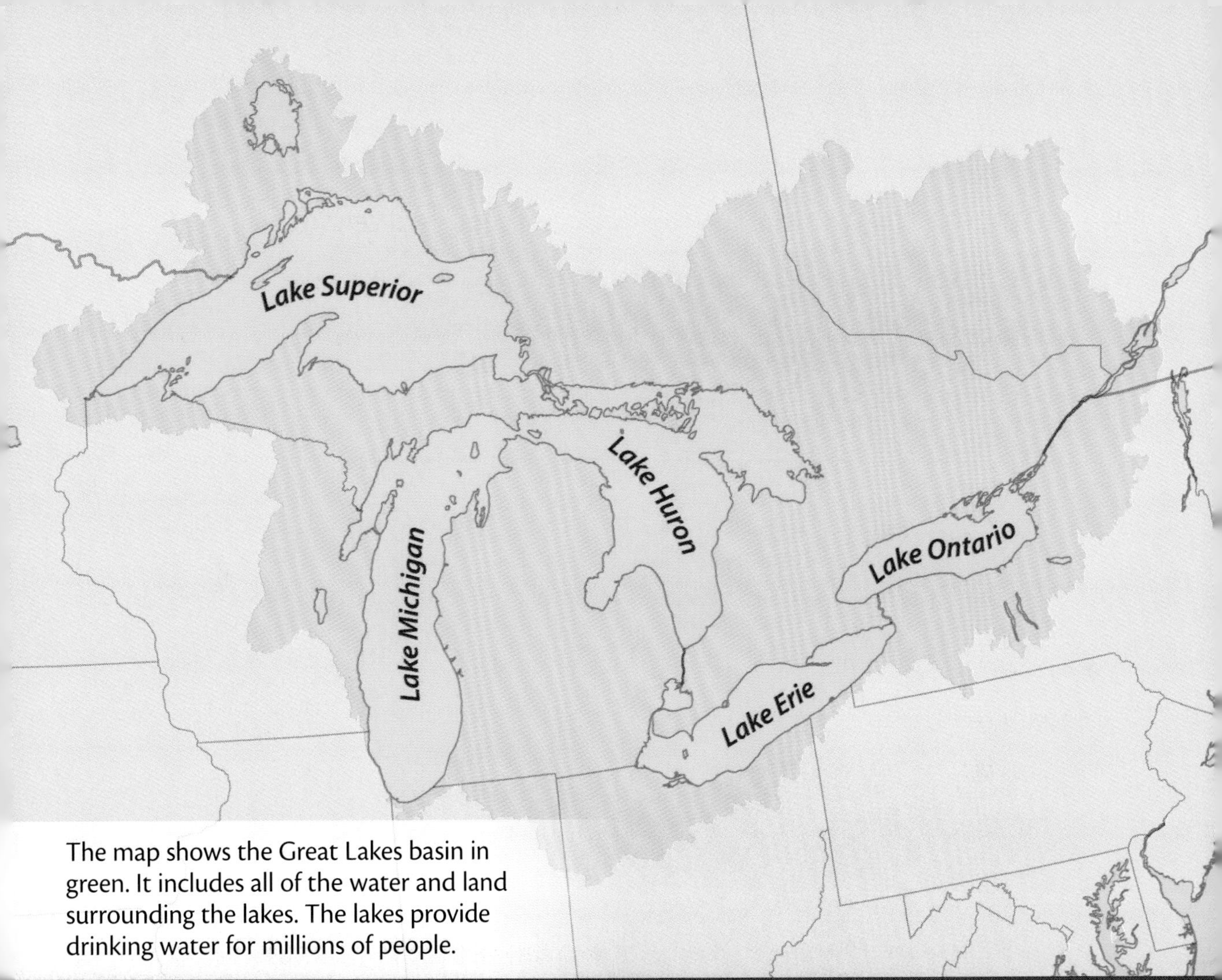


The map shows the Great Lakes basin in green. It includes all of the water and land surrounding the lakes. The lakes provide drinking water for millions of people.

## 14,000 YEARS AGO

The last glaciers slowly melted. Lake Michigan began to form. Deposition along the edge of the ice sheet helped trap water in the basin.

## 3,000 YEARS AGO TO PRESENT

Lake Michigan started to reach its present-day shape and size. It is the second-largest Great Lake. Water from four states drains into it.

## Mighty Glaciers, Many Lakes

Minnesota, Michigan, and Wisconsin have thousands of lakes. Many are the result of glaciers. As ice sheets slowly moved, they scraped the land like giant bulldozers. The ice piled soil and rock into tall ridges of sediment. It carved deep holes and left hills of rock. Low places filled with water from melting ice, forming the lakes.

Minnesota has more than 12,000 lakes.

Glaciers have come and gone several times in Minnesota. Melting glacial ice formed Minnesota's lakes about 8,000 years ago. Minnesota has more than 53,000 square kilometers (20,500 square miles) of surface water in its lakes, rivers, and wetlands. It's no wonder Minnesota is called "Land of 10,000 Lakes"!

# Rivers at Work

Like glaciers, the moving water in rivers is a mighty force of nature. Rivers shape the land through erosion and deposition. As rivers flow, they carve out valleys, cut **canyons,** and carry huge amounts of sediment. Where a river pours into a lake or ocean, it can build new land called a delta. You can't observe ice-age glaciers, but you can observe rivers at work.

A river delta in Lake Chiemsee, Germany

Most rivers start small. They grow larger by collecting water from rain and melting snow. Rivers also grow as smaller streams and rivers feed into them. No matter how big or small, all rivers flow downhill. The steepness of the slope controls how fast a river flows. The faster it flows, the more land it can erode. Rivers pick up large amounts of sediment by cutting into soil and rock. Rivers take the sediment to other areas, eventually forming new land, such as deltas.

# A Grand Landform

The Colorado River winds through the Grand Canyon. The river shaped the Grand Canyon through erosion and other processes. It carved the canyon into steep cliffs and gentle slopes.

The Colorado River began cutting into Earth's surface about five to six million years ago. The river cut downward. It carried rocks and boulders and wore away the rock walls. Today parts of the Grand Canyon are more than a mile deep!

**1,840–270**
**MILLION YEARS AGO**

Water and wind deposited new layers of sediment. The sediment layers gradually became rock layers.

The Colorado River flows along the bottom of the Grand Canyon.

## HOW DID THE GRAND CANYON FORM?

**70–40**
**MILLION YEARS AGO**

Forces below Earth's surface pushed up an area of land bigger than New Mexico. It was raised thousands of meters.

**5–6**
**MILLION YEARS AGO**

The Colorado River began to flow. The high elevation allowed the river to flow very fast. The river cut deeper into the rock.

**Present**

The Colorado continued eroding rock. Parts of the canyon walls fell inward. They were also eroded. Today the canyon is very deep and wide.

# The Mighty Mississippi

The Mississippi River is one of North America's largest and longest rivers. It flows from Minnesota's Lake Itasca to the Gulf of Mexico. The river is shallow enough to cross without a boat at Lake Itasca. Near the Gulf, the river is about 67 meters (200 feet) deep. How does it grow so large?

Many other rivers and streams empty into it. Even more water empties into the Mississippi during times of heavy rain. If the river gets too full, it flows onto the surrounding land, or floodplain.

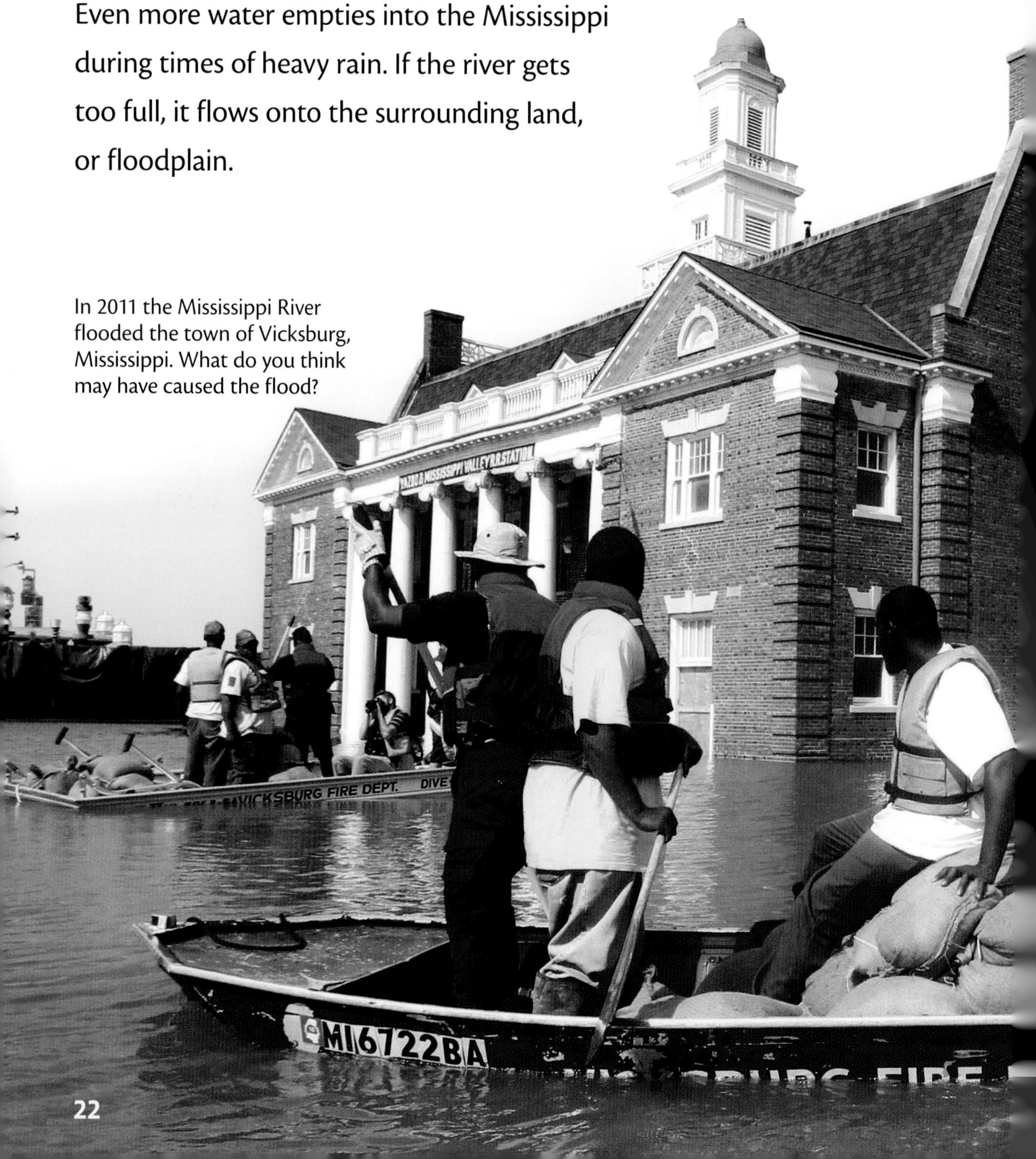


In 2011 the Mississippi River flooded the town of Vicksburg, Mississippi. What do you think may have caused the flood?

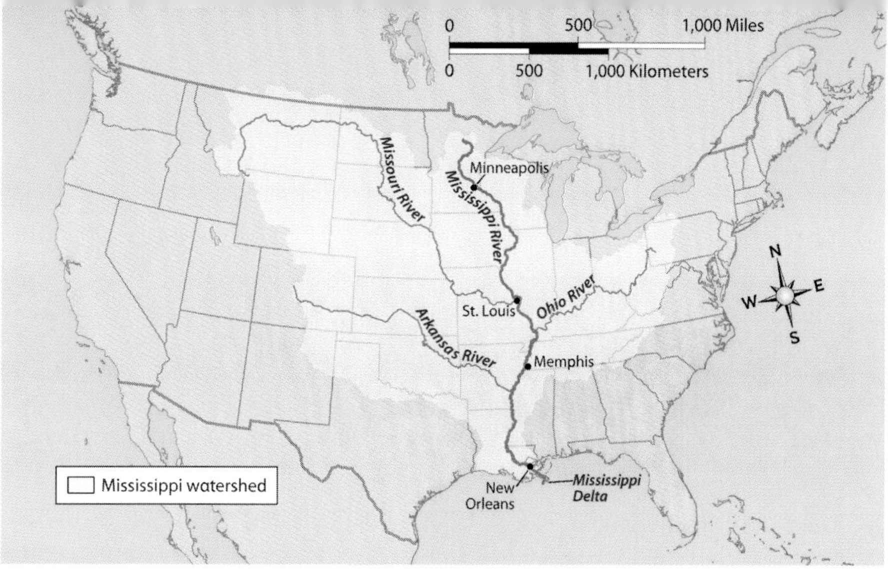


The Mississippi collects water from almost half of the United States.

The Mississippi has flooded many times. Each flood moves a lot of sediment. Places in the floodplain that are normally dry can be under water. Some places have been under more than 14 meters (45 feet) of water. Levees, or ridges of earth, protect nearby towns. If the Mississippi flows over the levees, the flooding can cause major damage.

Earth's water changes land through erosion, deposition, and the wearing away of rock. Signs of water's might are everywhere, from the Great Lakes to the Grand Canyon to the Mississippi River.

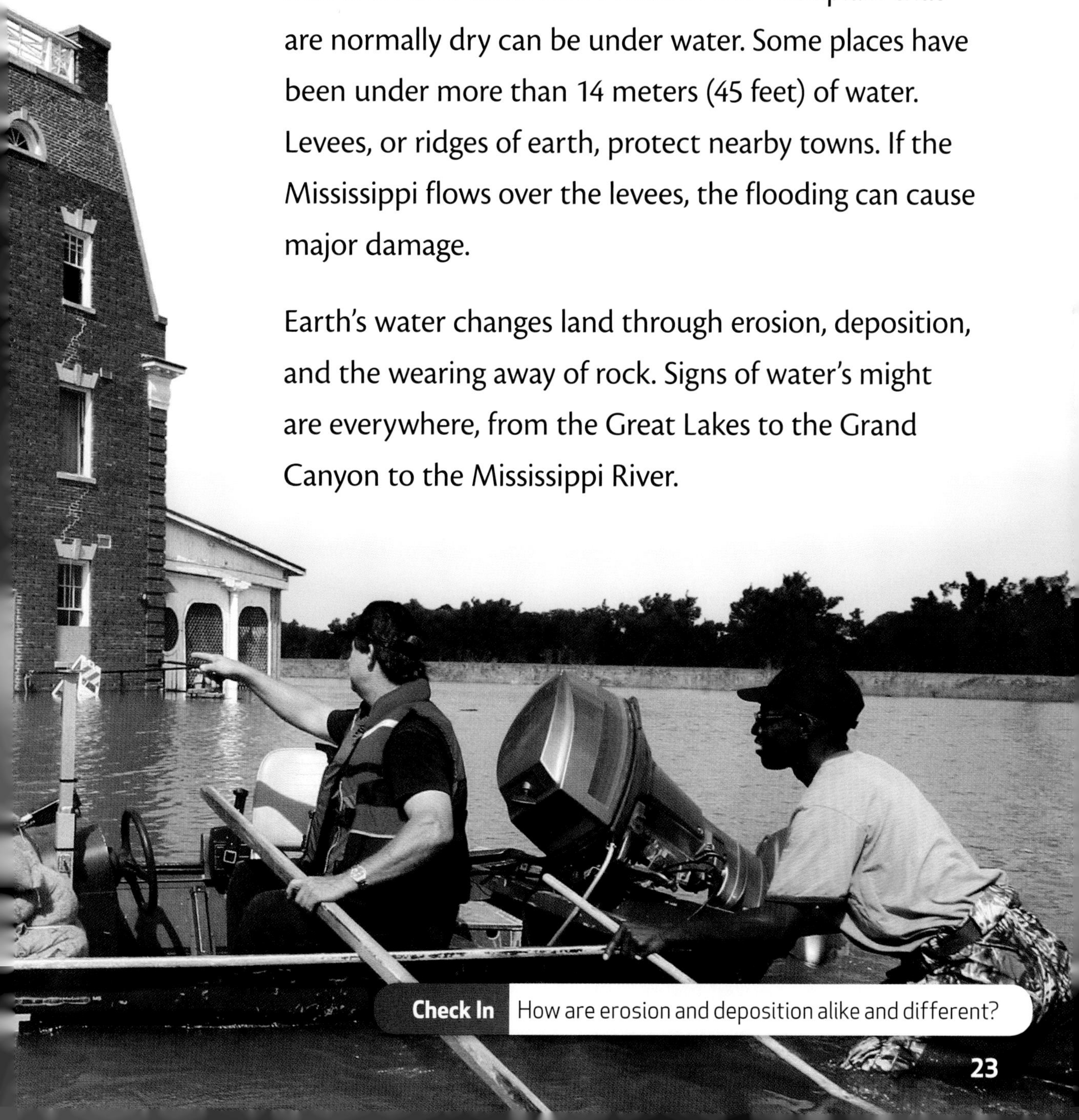

**Check In** How are erosion and deposition alike and different?

## Discuss Characters and Concepts

1. What do you think connects the two pieces that you read in this book? What makes you think that?

2. In "Paul Bunyan and Babe the Blue Ox," explain what events formed the Great Lakes.

3. What do you think is the most important idea in "Water's Might"? What makes you think that? Cite some supporting details.

4. About how long ago did the Colorado River begin to carve out the Grand Canyon? Cite evidence from the text to support your answer.

5. What do you still wonder about Earth's water or landforms? What would be some good ways to find more information?